FLIPPING
IN A *SNAP!*

A GUIDE TO
MAKING MONEY IN 30 DAYS OR LESS
WITH A **UNIQUE FLIPPING STRATEGY**

DREW LEVIN & DANNY PERKINS
Stars of TV's *"Renovate to Rent"*

FLIPPING IN A SNAP!: A GUIDE TO MAKING MONEY IN 30 DAYS OR LESS WITH A UNIQUE FLIPPING STRATEGY!

Contents

Introduction

Drew Levin and Danny Perkins here. We're excited about this book because it helps us to launch regular people like you in a business that anyone can start tomorrow. You will not need a bunch of cash, an office or any overhead.

We're the Renovate to Rent guys, but that isn't what this book is about. In our renovation and rental investing business we began to experience a slowing pipeline of the right properties for our business concept. It wasn't that they weren't out there. It was more that we were so busy with renovating and managing the rentals that we didn't have enough time to dig up the best properties. We were missing deals.

In an effort to fill our business funnel with great properties we came up with a concept that trained people to do our property location for us. It evolved into an exciting business strategy all its own... "Snap Flipping."

The beauty of business is that anytime there is a new concept that adds value, it becomes a business of its own because it is a win-win for the entrepreneurs. We had a need for more properties that met our detailed requirements.

In training others to locate and negotiate for those houses, we found that a whole new and exciting business opportunity was the result. We're just two guys and one investing business. There are thousands of other real estate investors out there with the same problem we had.

All of these active real estate investors, whether rental property buyers or fix & flip investors, were busy running their businesses and seeking out new properties to keep growing. If we needed help, then it is only logical that these other investors needed help as well.

Why not help others to become successful entrepreneurs doing snap flipping? They could deliver properties to us and many other investors. As the concept caught fire, it is being introduced around the country. We're thrilled that we have been instrumental in creating financial success for hundreds, and the list is growing.

What is snap flipping?

Snap flipping in its purest form is locating a real estate property and delivering it as-is to another real estate investor. The typical deal from end-to-end is finished in under 30 days, sometimes much faster. It requires little or no money from the snap flipper, and doesn't even require them to buy the property in order to sell it. The exciting high points:

- You don't need any licenses or permits.
- You don't have to buy real estate.
- You don't have to fix it up.
- You pass the transaction off sometimes as quickly as the same or next day.
- You get paid either when you pass the deal on or when it closes with your buyer, or a combination of the two.
- You set your fee, and your investor buyers gladly pay it to get the properties they want.

Our plan to train people to help us keep our property pipeline full quickly grew into a business of its own. Those who we were training quickly found that they could find properties that we didn't want but other investors would love to buy. They became successful entrepreneurs and now the concept is catching on around the country.

In this book you're going to get the full business plan, structure and process to become a successful snap flipper. We are also making available other resources and education to speed your business startup and enhance your profitability.

Read on to start your own business part time or full time with little or no money and no credit needed.

Chapter 1

What Snap Flipping is NOT

This photo helps us to explain our Snap Flipping process compared to the many house flipping shows on TV and the books about flipping a house with renovation. There are two ways to get burned in doing a standard flip with rehab; physically and financially. Let's take a look.

Maybe you've been to a few seminars, bought a course or two, and even been to a few actual homes under rehab. It's time to take your shot. You will be flipping a house to a rental home investor. You've done your homework, have a few rental buyers on your list, and you know what they want and roughly what they'll pay.

The Rehab Flip

The Standard Flip

You Buy It   Fix it Up   Sell it

Along with your flipping courses you also took a few contracting classes and bought several books on estimating remodel and repairs. You even have a couple of online tools to help you to calculate the cost of repairs, and you've practiced.

You've learned how to locate and vet contractors so you aren't doing the work yourself. The ways they are scheduled, controlled and paid are in your books and seminar information. If your goal is to have more than one snap flip going at a time, it is critical that you have your ducks in a row when it comes to contractors and job scheduling.

You have been scouring the area for the right house to flip and finally located a good candidate. It's a foreclosure that's been empty for almost a year, and it's in rough shape. Your competitors have been ignoring it because they don't see potential with the amount of rehab work that is necessary.

You watch this house in the foreclosure listings go through two price reductions, so it's time to act. You make a lowball offer that gets accepted simply because the bank is tired of holding the home and their costs to do so are rising. You end up getting it for 20% below the original foreclosure list price. It's a deal!

You have done your due diligence on local rents in the area, so you know from your preliminary number-crunching that this home can produce positive rental cash flow. The ARV, After Repair Value, of the house should be about $152,000. You know the rental buyer will not want to pay more than 85% of that, or about $129,200.

Your repair/rehab estimate comes to around $35,000, but you're careful so you make it $37,000. This includes preliminary bids from sub-contractors. Now you're at $129,200 - $37,000 = $92,200. You're a genius and a great negotiator, getting this house for $79,900, all costs of sale included. There's a cool $12,300 in it, but you think you can hit your initial rehab estimate and do even better. You're on your way to being a flipping guru!

Ah, but you have to fund the purchase and rehab. You've taken out a transaction funding loan, and if you finish on time, you'll have to pay $3,700 to the lender as interest and fees. That's OK though, as you still have more than $8,600 or more for your profit, not bad for a month's work.

Only, that month turns into two months due to some problems in the rehab. Along with one slow subcontractor, there was some hidden termite damage and there were beams to be replaced. That adds to the cost of the rehab, and the delay adds to the interest and fees owed the transaction lender.

In trying to recoup some of these added costs, you decide to jump in and do some of the work yourself. It seemed simple to check the existing wiring and make repairs. Our photo is how you looked when you turned on the breakers and started shaking and pulling wires in the crawlspace. It seems there had been some rodent damage to the wiring insulation.

So, you've been burned in the literal sense, and you let the electrical contractor take over. When it's all said and done, your buyer closes on the deal at their desired price, as you can't talk them up. Your transaction lender is paid off and their fees paid. You leave the closing table with $2,800 +/- for your 2+ months' work and your risk. Now you've been burned twice.

Not terrible, as you're happy it wasn't any worse. However, now you wonder if you even want to take a stab at a second deal. Maybe some more study, a few more courses and seminars, but that's going to cost you too. The good news is that there is another way to flip houses and avoid most of the risk and all of the rehab headaches.

The Snap Flip

The Snap Flip

You Buy It   Fix it Up   Sell it

No, we didn't mess up this image. With our Snap Flip process, you're going to be able to completely avoid the purchase and the rehab, and you'll still pocket a nice fee at the closing table… or sooner!

You're just changing your buyer customer type. Now you will be selling the home to a fix & flip investor. They will in turn sell it to a retail customer or a rental investor. They're going to take those first two items off your plate.

Wait! You can't sell a home you don't own! Yes, you can. A simple wording change in a purchase agreement, the same one used to buy the home, will get the job done. It's an "assignment" clause and a small change in the "Buyer" identifier box.

In this book, we're going to give you specific information about how snap flipping works. It is a process by which you "gain control" of a property rather than buying it. You then pass your control over to your buyer for your fee. You may be able to collect all or a part of your fee when you pass over control, but, if not, you will get paid at the closing table when your buyer settles the purchase.

You're going to learn who the players are in the snap flip process, the motivations of each and most of all, your value to the others. You do not enter the snap flip as a sales person or a hustler trying to take advantage of anyone. Your role is one that allows you to help a seller to move a problem property, and to help a fix & flip or rental buyer to purchase a great investment.

Forget getting burned by problems and delays in the rehab process and maybe burned literally if you take an active role in the fixing to save money and get back on the budget. You're about to learn a clean, low risk and profitable process that puts money in your pocket, usually in 30 days or faster.

Chapter 2

The Players – Investor Buyers

If you take away only one thing from this chapter, understand that your buyer and source of your business profit is not buying a house; they're buying an investment. This doesn't matter whether your investor buyer is going to fix & flip the house or they're a ready-to-rent rental property investor.

They are buying an investment. Sure, they care about the looks of the home and its features, but only from the perspective of their buyer or potential tenant. It is all about money, cash flow and ultimate profit. If you want to walk through a home and point out the beautiful kitchen and the great workshop, then get a real estate license and work with retail home buyers.

Starting at the Last Step

Why are we starting this discussion on the tail end of the process? The sale comes at the end, so why not start at the beginning where we're looking for a house to snap flip?

One of the biggest draws for our snap flipping strategy and process is that you turn a nice profit in a very short period of time. The other major draw is that you can do it with little or no cash out of your pocket.

It's the speed at which these deals move through the process that makes if critical that you have the last step covered before you ever start the first step. You MUST have a buyer, or more than one, lined up. If you don't, you'll waste time and maybe money locking up a house with nowhere to deliver it.

In a future chapter we'll go over the ways in which you can locate buyer prospects. You will learn to develop a list of them, a database of sorts. You'll record their contact information, but also some important facts to help you in delivering a house they will want to buy:

- Neighborhoods of interest
- House characteristics of interest
- Price range (ARV, after repair value)

Once you have this data recorded with each buyer, you have the information you need to seek out houses you're going to be able to move in a hurry. You have to know who your buyers are and what they want before you go out and find deals. Otherwise you could be wasting a lot of effort and maybe some money on houses that you can't sell.

We're going to talk about two types of buyers, fix & flip and rental property investors. The fix & flip investors are ultimately probably going to sell to a rental property buyer.

In the crash that started in 2006, for the first few years there were so many foreclosures that you could often find one vacant only for a short time. It may be in good condition, ready to rent. However, as foreclosures dropped off beginning in 2010, the majority of them are pretty damaged, having been vacant sometimes for a year or more.

For this reason you're more likely to be working with a fix & flip buyer, but you never know when you'll come across a house in decent condition, so we'll talk about the rental house buyer too.

The Rental House Buyer

You're working with a buyer who may be willing to do some minor cosmetic work on the home to get it ready for a tenant. However, they'll want it to be minor and able to be done very quickly. They're not making money until the home has a tenant in it.

You build your buyer list and categorize these as rental investor buyers, recording their preferences for neighborhoods, house characteristics and price ranges. Later we'll go over their specific due diligence process, how they determine what a house will rent for, their requirements for cash flow and the numbers of the deal.

The single most important success factor working with these investor buyers is to deliver them houses that meet their specifications and will generate the cash flow they want at current prevailing rents. And they will want to buy the home below current market value, as that's every investor's goal.

The Fix & Flip Investor

You're going to have more opportunities to find houses that need work, sometimes extensive work, before they can be sold to a rental home buyer.

This situation came about as the massive foreclosure glut began to die down. It is also in part dependent upon whether the state in which you're investing is a judicial or non-judicial foreclosure state.

Non-judicial Foreclosure State

In these states the courts are not normally involved in foreclosures. A deed of trust is executed at the time of the purchase. The trustee holds the deed until all mortgage payments are made as agreed.

If a borrower goes into default, according to the time frames indicated by that state's laws, the trustee is allowed to foreclose and sell the property, and evict the borrower if necessary.

This is normally an efficient process that gets the property off the lender's books within 120 days or so from the foreclosure filing.

States Using Non-judicial Foreclosure

Alabama	Nebraska
Alaska	Nevada
Arizona	New Hampshire
Arkansas	New Mexico (sometimes)
California	North Carolina
Colorado	Oklahoma
D.C.	Oregon
Georgia	Rhode Island
Idaho	South Dakota
Maryland	Tennessee
Massachusetts	Texas
Michigan	Utah
Minnesota	Virginia
Mississippi	Washington
Missouri	West Virginia
Montana	Wyoming

There are some of these states that allow the homeowner to request judicial foreclosure.

Judicial Foreclosure State

In these states, foreclosures go through the court system. The lender files the documents with the court in the time frames specified in that state's laws. Lawyers and judges are involved, including hearings and more filings and documents.

This process takes significantly longer. After the early foreclosure abuses in 2007 and 2008, the courts became more observant and more careful in examining documents and holding lenders to the letter of the law.

If there are any document problems or delaying tactics on one side or the other, these foreclosures can easily take a year or even much longer to work their way through the process.

States using Judicial Foreclosure

Connecticut	Delaware
Florida	Hawaii
Illinois	Indiana
Iowa	Kansas
Kentucky	Louisiana
Maine	New Jersey
New Mexico (mostly)	New York
North Dakota	Ohio
Oklahoma	Pennsylvania
South Carolina	Vermont
Wisconsin	

In some of these states the delays and court process have caused homes to remain empty for a year or more routinely. In these cases their condition can be pretty bad if vandalized while vacant.

Delivery in As-Is Condition

You will be delivering these houses to a fix & flip investor in an as-is condition. You're not going to do anything to them.

You will already know what local rental property buyers have for criteria for their investments, and this fix & flip buyer will have the same information. This buyer will have their own buyer list. Your selling price must allow for the costs of rehab and a profit to the fix & flip buyer, plus a discount to their rental property buyer.

This means being able to estimate their rehab costs as closely as possible. Knowing what they can sell a home for and what it will cost them to rehab it will give you the number you must meet if you're going to get them to buy the house you deliver.

Better Math than Rehab!

Here's your first exposure to the awesome advantages of the snap flipping strategy. You're not going to care about the condition of the home. Yes, you will need to take it into consideration and estimate rehab costs your fix & flip investor will encounter. But, you don't have to take the time, effort and risk of doing the repairs and rehab. They're going to buy it just like it sits!

Chapter 3

The Players – Sellers

The other end of your snap flipping pipeline is the seller. Here is where you have a more diverse set of prospects. With the different prospect types come very different negotiation strategies. You may be locating a home that:

1. Has a homeowner occupant with default notices wanting to avoid foreclosure.
2. A homeowner who needs to sell in a hurry to relocate or due to family or medical problems.
3. A divorce situation with a need to sell to split the proceeds, and it is time sensitive.
4. An estate sale liquidating the assets of the deceased.
5. A bank owned foreclosure property.

Depending on your market area and the current economic and employment conditions, you'll find that one or more of these prospective situations will present more opportunities than others.

What will change with different situations will be your negotiation strategies and your value to the sellers in the transaction. Let's talk about that "value" component.

You are going to succeed at snap flipping if you understand that you can deliver great value not only to your buyers but also to sellers. Both are trying to accomplish something, and your value is in helping them to do so.

For sellers, they need to sell a home. For whatever reasons, they cannot take the regular route of listing with a real estate agent on the retail market. Whether it's time sensitive or money related, they haven't been able to get rid of that home. Your value, IF THE NUMBERS WORK, is in helping them to get rid of that home weighting them down or keeping them from moving on.

That thing about the numbers working is critical. You will have to do your due diligence into what the home is worth or will be worth after rehab. You'll have to know what they owe on mortgages and if there are any liens against the property.

If you've done your buyer due diligence first, you know approximately what you can sell the home for, so now it's just calculating whether it's possible to get to a purchase number that gives you the profit you want to go forward with the deal.

The first thing you do is to come to the number you can work with for a purchase price and see whether there is room to pay off the house and get it for that number. If not, you may still want to work through a short sale, especially if there isn't a lot of room to make up.

Even if there is enough equity in the home for your offer to get the owner out from under, they may not want to move on with little or nothing in their pocket after closing. That's just part of the negotiation process. You're not there to beat them up. You simply explain that your business will not allow you to pay more than $X for the home because your buyer is in control of the ultimate resolution. If there is sufficient equity the situation is the simplest, as your seller needs only to decide just how badly the want or need to sell. You're delivering a solution to their problem at the only price that will work. The ball is in their court.

If they do not have enough equity, you may see enough potential in the ultimate deal to work through a short sale process with their lender. However, this really takes away the whole "snap" in snap flipping, so it would really take a great bargain basement ultimate purchase price to go through the hassle. For this snap flipping concept, it's really best to just tell the seller you can't be of help.

The Distressed or Hurried Seller With Equity

These are prospects 1 and 2 in our list above. Assuming that there is enough equity in the home to get it for your price and pay off the mortgages and liens, it's a simple negotiation. You should, from the first contact with these sellers, present yourself as someone who helps homeowners in their situation by connecting them to investor or other buyers who can buy their home quickly and for cash.

You are there hoping that you can help within the limitations of your business model. If they see that you truly want to help, they are unlikely to get upset at your offer price. They may not want to sell for that (at least not that day), but they understand that you have buyers and they set the monetary rules. Who knows, if you part on good terms, they may just decide that they have no other choice and call you back a week or so later.

The Divorce Situation

Most divorces that require the selling of the house to split assets will list with a real estate broker. However, if there is just enough equity to pay that sales commission with little left over to split, then perhaps they'll respond to an offer that will get them cash in a hurry. You're still going to offer a price that likely will leave little or nothing to split, but they can move the house quicker for cash and get out of each other's life.

If your numbers work for one of your buyers and a decent profit for you, then this could be a good deal for all involved.

Up to now we've been dealing with occupied homes that are probably in good condition and you'll be working with a rental property investor. This gives you a little more room to negotiate and make some money.

The Estate

A personal representative or other estate trustee will be tasked with selling the assets of a deceased person to pay off their debts and divide any money left among the heirs. Often this person is a relative or other non-compensated party designated in the will. They're taking time away from their lives and will want to get the liquidation process finished without a lot of delay.

Of course, they will be trying to maximize the sale proceeds on behalf of the deceased and the heirs, but they do want things to move along. The commissions involved in listing the home will be a consideration, so you may be able to construct an offer without a listing agent involved that will work for everyone involved.

The main concern here for you is the condition of the home. Sometimes they are in excellent condition, so you're working with a rental home buyer. However, if the deceased let the home deteriorate in their later years, then you need to run your numbers for sale to a fix & flip investor.

Depending on your location and the local county's adoption of the Internet for records, you may be able to locate these properties online. However, often you'll take the death notices from the paper and have to research the county records to see if real estate is involved.

The Bank Owned Property

Once a property has worked its way through the foreclosure process, it is going on the auction block. You should check out online resources for auctions and notices. In the heyday of foreclosures after the bust, some investors did quite well, buying homes at 50% or better discounts off value at the auctions.

However, the lender is there to bid as well. The lender isn't going to let you or any other bidder take a home for a song if they believe they can market it and get more of their investment back.

However, here's where what you don't know can help you make a good deal. You have no idea of what percentage of assets on the lender's books are non-performing at that time. If they're approaching some limits that will cause them problems with other parts of their business or in issuing new loans, they may just want the home gone.

It's easy to just bid low and get it, but that's not how you stay out of the poor house. You must get enough advance notice of the auction to do some due diligence on the homes out for bid. At least a drive-by and cursory valuation is in order. As you get better at snap flipping and learn your market area, you'll be able to do some pretty accurate valuations to get ready for auctions.

However, a large percentage of auctions end up with the lender buying the property. They then list it for sale with the plan to recoup as much of their investment as possible.

The good news is that your exposure at the auction gives you information about this home as to what you find it is worth to you and what the lender will be trying to sell it for. You can just watch that listing to see what happens. If it sits there a while, one or more price reductions are likely. At some point it may reach the magic number you need for a deal.

If a home is in rugged condition, it's more likely that the lender will let it go at auction. However, your ability to inspect the property is limited, so you want to be very careful. If condition is rough, shooting for a VERY deep discount to ARV, After Repair Value, is the approach to take.

Your purchase at auction is without any recourse for problems with the property, so you'll want to do as much due diligence as possible as to title, liens and condition before holding up that bidding card.

Locating Potential Deals

This is where you'll spend a lot of time and effort, and it is almost always worth every bit of it. One major component of your value to your buyers is your ability to find deals they cannot find or are unwilling to dig enough to locate them.

You'll want to learn more and do your own online and offline research, but let's go through the most productive ways in which you will be able to locate profitable deals before the competition.

The Bandit Sign

You've seen these signs stuck in the ground on street corners or nailed to light poles. They are placed by investors who want to get the attention of homeowners in the neighborhood as they drive by. Various wordings work:

- I Buy Houses – Any Condition
- We Buy Houses for Cash FAST
- Avoid Foreclosure – We'll Buy Your House Cash
- Cash FAST for Your House

The idea is to get the distressed homeowner to notice the sign every day until they need your services, and they'll call the number on the sign.

Classified Ads

Classified ads are inexpensive and they do work, but only if run consistently in the same categories in the classified section over time. People who may have no need to sell their home now will read these ads, see them again and again, and at some point they will need help and remember that ad and call.

Craigslist

Craigslist, even with the scams that are common on the site, provides a great free opportunity to search for motivated sellers.

Here are three of numerous results in a search in houses for sale for the words "must sell."

☆ Oct 29 Must Sell FAST! 3br - (PASADENA) pic map ⌧

☆ Nov 7 MUST SELL Super Deal. $65k. Cash Only $65 4br - 1200ft² - (Houston) pic map ⌧

☆ Nov 4 3 fixer upper houses must sell (Houston/Galveston area) map ⌧

You'll find flippers advertising with these words, but you'll also find the occasional distressed homeowner listing their home. It's an easy introduction because they're seeking you out.

☆ $74950 Fixer upper home for sale by owner houston texas (5622 Gaston

Reduced price is $74, 950. and take care of any and all fees and or taxes, and any other amount owed concerning this property, includes past and present and future fees, since I'm reducing price, the buyer can be responsible.
Was asking $98,999 but will sell today for $74,950 plus pay what I owe. im doing this offer, because I need cash this week, we would like to buy a newer truck, so whoever can buy my property this week, is the winner that gets this great deal.
If buyer is interested, then we would also consider an all cash deal $74,950 but call me for more details, just call me if interested in buying my house and land, I'm the owner and here is my number (show contact info) call or text.

• do NOT contact me with unsolicited services or offers

That's another ad found searching around with various key words related to distressed sellers seeking cash buyers fast. It could be a great deal if accurate.

Foreclosure Websites

Realtytrac.com is a large site dedicated to home auctions, pre-foreclosures and foreclosures. You'll find other sites just searching Google for "foreclosure homes."

Old Fashioned Networking

Get some business cards printed up and let everyone you know that you're a real estate investor who specializes in helping sellers out of their homes for cash.

Get to know some real estate agents. When they bump into someone who can't list their home but needs to sell (maybe owe too much or in a big hurry), you want them to send them your way.

It really doesn't matter how you find a potential deal. Every tool and resource you use increases your chance and business profitability.

Chapter 4

The Players - You

To take on your role in this business, it is important to understand your value to the two other players. We've talked about building your buyer list and learning what your buyers want for investment properties, whether rental investors or fix & flip investors. Only by knowing how they evaluate their investments can you deliver houses to them that will be quickly scooped up.

As for sellers, we talked about distressed sellers, those who may need to move in a hurry and can't take the time to list their homes. Others are facing foreclosure and would like to avoid it. Or, you're dealing with the lenders and asset managers unloading bank owned foreclosure properties.

The Seller's Puzzle

Those owner occupants who need to sell have a pretty simple puzzle. They have a home they either can't afford, are about to lose to foreclosure or that they need to unload in a hurry to move for a job or life change.

They may have tried the listing route, or they talked to real estate agents and found that it wouldn't work for them financially or quickly enough for their needs. Their puzzle is finding someone to just take their home off their backs, usually knowing they're going to get little or nothing when they leave the closing table.

You're marketing and prospecting and these people call or email you hoping you can help. Usually when it gets to this stage, they know they will take a beating on price, but that is secondary to getting out from under the home.

It is critical that you understand your role, and the fact that you're not at their kitchen table to SELL them anything or to force them into a sale. You should think of yourself more as a problem-solver, there to see if you can help them to get that home sold.

In your discussions, you can be clear that your business is all about finding a willing investor buyer to pay cash and do it in a hurry. You can tell them that you have a group of buyers who rely upon you to locate rental or rehab properties for them.

The questions you ask and the numbers you crunch are all about seeing if you can help them to solve their puzzle by matching their home up with an investor with ready cash. If the numbers work, there will be a top line you can pay, no more, as your buyer sets the rules.

If your numbers work for them, then you can execute an assignment contract that you will present to your buyer(s) to match them up and get the home sold in a short period of time, usually 30 days or sooner.

If the numbers do not work for either you or the seller, then there will not be a deal. Keeping it on this business level should avoid any hard feelings on their part when you're unable to help. If you can't find that missing piece to solve their puzzle, it's unfortunate but that's business.

The Buyer's Puzzle

Your investor buyers, whether fix & flip or rental property investors have a simple need; they just want viable investments to grow their businesses. It's a simple need, but not simple to fill. If it was, you wouldn't have value to add or a business.

The more you know about your buyers' requirements the better you will be able to deliver properties you can be reasonably sure that they will buy, or even compete over. In our chapter about your buyer list, we made it clear that you must know buyer due diligence processes, what they'll pay and the type of houses they want.

You become the puzzle piece in the middle that solves both of their puzzles. You are adding value to the transaction, as it would never have happened had you not set up your business and processes to identify buyers and locate properties to deliver to them that fit their investment goals.

The amazing thing about our snap flipping concept is that once you are set up, have buyers and start locating properties, you're going to roll these deals in less than 30 days in most cases. Sometimes you'll be able to close the transaction in a couple of weeks or so if the due diligence into the title chain for the property is successfully completed.

What About Setting Up?

Starting out you still must be serious about operating as a business. How you structure your business is up to you, but you should at least think about formal business structures at this point.

Sole Proprietor

The clear majority of new entrepreneurs start out in the sole proprietorship business structure. You're operating in your name, and for all practical and financial purposes, you and your business are a single entity.

The advantages are simplicity and minor government regulation. Often you do not need a permit of any type to operate in your residence, and for income taxes there is a separate schedule on your personal return for your business reporting.

The drawback is primarily liability. Everything you own is at risk should your business create a financial failure or if you get sued for something you allegedly do in your business.

The good news is that it is usually not a major problem to convert your business structure later as you grow and find that you would like to minimize liability or change how your business taxes are handled.

Partnership

This is a structure used when multiple owners active in the business want to share ownership as modified sole proprietors.

Liability for the debts and operations of the partnership is borne by the partners in relation to their share of ownership. Profits are treated the same as in a sole proprietorship, taxed on the personal returns of the partners.

This is the simplest structure for multiple owners, and it is often used as a temporary business entity for real estate projects, such as the construction of a shopping mall.

The Full C Corporation

This is usually the structure used by larger companies, and it shields shareholders from liability and any debt obligations of the company. The shareholders receive dividends on their stock holdings and benefit from an increase in share value if operations are effective.

The biggest drawback is double taxation. The corporation pays tax on income and when the shareholders receive profits, they pay taxes on the same money again through their personal returns. Another drawback is boatloads of paperwork and requirements for shareholder meetings and operations.

Subchapter S Corporation

This is a popular structure as it has the best of both the sole proprietorship and the C corporations. The shareholder(s), often just the owner(s), are shielded from liability for corporate debt and business practice liability. However, the profits of the business are taxed only once when they are passed through to the shareholder(s).

There are some requirements for how the business is operated and shareholder activities that come with the S corporation, but they're far less of a hassle than those of a C corporation.

The LLC

There are some variations as to how a Limited Liability Company (LLC) is structured and is operated. However, what it does is a bit like the S Corporation, limiting the liability of owners, as the assets of the LLC itself are all that become available to satisfy debts or a lawsuit judgement.

Profits are passed through without double taxation, with the owner/shareholders reporting them on their personal returns.

Don't let it become a drag at first.

Sure, discussing this with your accountant may influence your startup, but taking the sole proprietor route is the easy, low/no paperwork option that can be changed later if your business takes off.

Overhead & Operations

This can and usually should be as simple as a computer and your kitchen table. Sure, if you want a home office, it's a tax break and you should do it if you have the room.

Information Storage & Retrieval

At this point you've learned that a database of buyers with details of their requirements is a necessary step. You can do this on index cards in a card box file, but most of us have a computer and the ability to store more information easily and find it when we need it.

Not only for buyers, you'll also want to store information about prospective properties, some listed on the local MLS, Multiple Listing Service.

You will be doing value calculations to determine what a property is worth now and after repairs, ARV, After Repair Value. You may watch some of these properties for a while, waiting for possible price reductions that will make them a possible deal.

Don't Get Complicated

The new entrepreneur can get too much into the mechanics of doing business and managing it, taking time away from the activities that generate profits. If you're spending more time in recording and retrieving information than in networking for buyers and negotiating with sellers, you're inefficient.

Keep it Mobile Friendly

A lot of your research will be done in the field, checking out properties and neighborhoods. You'll be using your smart phone then instead of your computer back at the kitchen table. There are many database and software products out there that can do a good job for you. However, the top three big players that bring it all together are:

Microsoft OneNote

Create your way

Do you scribble great ideas on napkins and sticky notes? Is precise filing more your style? OneNote's got you covered whatever way you shape your thoughts. Type, write or draw with the free form feel of pen to paper. Search and clip from the web to picture ideas.

Google Keep

When and where you need it

Need to remember to pick up some groceries? Set a location-based reminder to pull up your grocery list right when you get to the store. Need to finish a to-do? Set a time-based reminder to make sure you never miss a thing.

Evernote

Make a note of it

Create a project to-do list. Jot down a reminder. Or snap a picture of a sketch. A note can be anything you want it to be. And once you make a note, it's accessible wherever you go, forever.

You can evaluate each at their respective sites, but to get to a thorough review and comparison, here is a quote from *PC World's* article:

"Google Keep, Microsoft OneNote, and Evernote each offer distinctive benefits. Unless you're Google-focused or Microsoft-centric, however, Evernote is the most diverse and capable service.

Google Keep is nice and simple, but its capabilities are extremely limited.

OneNote is an exceptional product, and comes in a close second to Evernote. Although OneNote is available for a variety of platforms and devices, it's still a Microsoft tool, so it lacks the platform-agnostic approach and strong third-party support that strengthen Evernote."

Using one of these applications will allow you to do everything from saving photos of houses with realtor signs out front, to saving copies of receipts for your accounting and keeping all your information on buyers.

It will become a fast and easy way to gather and retrieve information using your computer or your smart phone in the field. **Keep it simple.**

You're ready, so go for it!

Chapter 5

Find Those Buyers

Now you have a basic business setup plan and you can move forward with it. The first step is to get that buyer list/database going. Without willing buyers, you have no need to go out and locate houses. What are some of the things you can do to build a strong investor buyer list?

Join a Real Estate Investment Club

Networking is a powerful business-building tool in every business. Real estate investment clubs are all around the country, and they are not only a great place to meet other investors, but also a place to learn a lot about our business.

Most investment clubs maintain training libraries of books, audio and video courses. They also invite guest speakers to share their knowledge, including people in related industries like mortgages, real estate brokerage, contracting and others.

To locate a club or group near you, here are three websites that have links to local clubs by state:

- CREOnline.com
- REIClub.com
- National Real Estate Investors Association

Most of them will let you attend a meeting to check them out before joining.

In these groups you will meet active investors, some of them great potential fix & flip and rental investors you can sell homes to in the future.

Many courses and books are telling new investors to join these clubs, so your membership can be an ongoing source for prospective buyers. Catching a new fix & flip or rental property buyer is going to be a great addition to your buyer list.

Classifieds & Craigslist

You can advertise for investor buyers. They are actively seeking houses, so they read classified ads too. First, you DO NOT need a house in hand to run ads to attract buyers.

Learn something about neighborhoods of interest to investors and the house prices there. You don't need to choose an actual house, instead a set of characteristics. You may run an ad starting with "Investor special" or "Must sell fixer-upper." State the area and the basic house characteristics for bedrooms, baths, etc. Put an appealing price on it for an investor.

WHEN you get a call or email, apologize saying you just put it under contract with another investor. But, you are working on a couple of others and would love to take down this investor's information so you can get in touch when you get a deal together.

Craigslist

Craigslist is online classifieds, and the huge advantage is that they are "searchable." Using keywords and phrases, you can use

Craigslist to build your buyer list.

Run ads like the one above in the classifieds. Use keywords like "must sell," "investors," "fixer-upper," etc. This will attract investor buyers you can add to your list.

Foreclosure Auctions

You don't necessarily have to be buying a house at a foreclosure auction. You can be there just to meet other investors. Often rental property investors and fix & flip investors are there. They may be competition at that auction, but they can become buyer customer prospects before they leave.

Using the Internet

The Internet has become the largest marketing and information sharing network in the world. There are sites where you can contact real estate investors in your area to add to your buyer list. Another benefit is that there are out-of-area investors who would invest in an area if they can cultivate relationships.

LinkedIn

LinkedIn is a social network focused on business. More than 450 million members all actively seeking to make business contacts makes this a great place to build a profile.

When you set up your profile, use the keywords and phrases related to real estate investment, fix & flip and rental property investing. Your profile will also highlight your business market area.

Post about what you do, deals you've completed and opportunities you are evaluating. Also join investor groups.

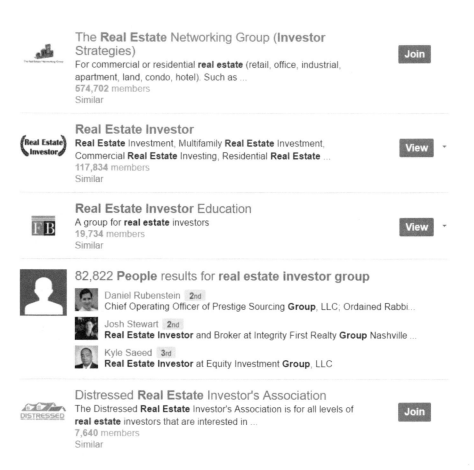

Notice the tens of thousands of people results related to a search on real estate investment groups. This level of involvement is free, so take advantage of it.

Facebook

Facebook is more of a social network, but you can build a business page there for free.

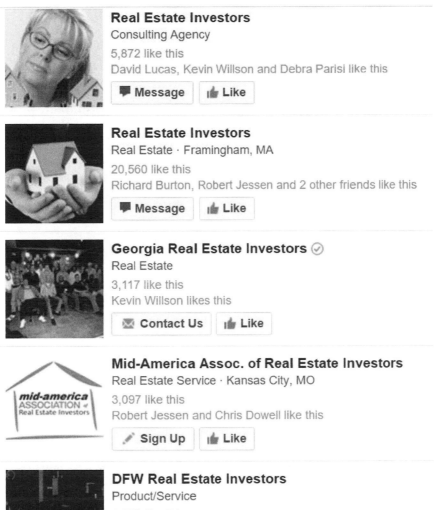

Real Estate Investors
Consulting Agency
5,872 like this
David Lucas, Kevin Willson and Debra Parisi like this

[Message] [Like]

Real Estate Investors
Real Estate · Framingham, MA
20,560 like this
Richard Burton, Robert Jessen and 2 other friends like this

[Message] [Like]

Georgia Real Estate Investors ⊘
Real Estate
3,117 like this
Kevin Willson likes this

[Contact Us] [Like]

Mid-America Assoc. of Real Estate Investors
Real Estate Service · Kansas City, MO
3,097 like this
Robert Jessen and Chris Dowell like this

[Sign Up] [Like]

DFW Real Estate Investors
Product/Service
1,070 like this
Gena Horiatis likes this

You'll find groups and discussions in your local area and nationally. One advantage is your ability to do some really inexpensive marketing on Facebook. For a tiny budget that you set, you can target ads to appear only to those on Facebook who have indicated real estate or real estate investment as interests in their profiles.

You can point that ad at your Facebook page, or as we'll talk about in this next section, your own website/blog.

Your Own Web Presence

Once you're up and running and want to take your marketing up a notch, you can build your own website/blog and it can be totally free.

Using WordPress.com as your resource, you can build out a site on free WordPress software hosted at that site. This is where you can get into more detail about what you do, your market area, and talk about deals you've put together.

When you run those Facebook ads, you can point them to your site rather than your Facebook page.

Become a Resource for Wannabe Investors

If you like people and helping them, you can advertise that you want to help new investors to get started. You're cultivating buyers for your list by helping them to get started. It can be as simple as getting together and letting them ask questions to a more structured seminar approach.

Back to Basics – Business Cards

Never undervalue the business building power of just handing out business cards to virtually everyone you meet. This is especially true of getting to know many real estate agents. They are active in the market and sometimes find deals that will not fit into the standard listing model. If they think you may be able to help, you'll get a lead. They also work with real estate investors.

Categorize Your Buyers

When you're taking notes and getting your buyer requirements, be organized and ask the same questions of all of them. When you record this information, you can then use one of the note taking and database solutions to pull them up when you have a house to deliver.

An example would be by neighborhood of interest. Querying your notes for "investors" and the neighborhood will get you to the best prospects for a property quickly.

Snap flipping is like an assembly line. You find the deal and move it along the line to the proper boxes, buyers interested in just that type of property and area.

The more buyers you put on your list the greater your ability to match one or more of them to each property. When they're bidding against each other for latest deal, you've made it!

Chapter 6

Understanding Your Buyers'
Due Diligence

Before you can deliver a house with certainty to an investor buyer, you need to know what the buyer wants and how they do their valuation and due diligence to make purchase decisions.

If for no other reason, your peace of mind and confidence when sealing the deal on your buying end will be much greater if you're sure you have one or more buyers who will want this house. You know what to offer and can go to your database and find one or more buyers who will want this house at a price that yields your desired investment profit result.

We're working primarily with two main customer types, the fix & flip investor and the rental property investor. The condition of the house you locate determines which you'll seek out to buy it.

We're going to start with the rental property buyer because everything they use in evaluating a property must be considered by the fix & flip investor as well. That's because the fix & flip investor is usually selling to a rental investor, so they need to know what they want and how they do their valuation.

Rental Property Investor Due Diligence

First, we're going to assume that the rental property buyer wants a house ready to rent or in need of only minor cosmetic corrections to make it ready. This will leave the rehab calculations to the fix & flip investor.

The rental property buyer has these main factors used in making their decision:

- What the property will rent for in the current market without rent concessions.
- The age and overall condition of the property to estimate improvements or major repairs that may become necessary during ownership.
- The cost they must pay related to the current market value; they want a discount.
- The prospect of value appreciation over time.

Let's take these one at a time so that you know what you must consider in making deal decisions.

Rents in the Current Market

The rental property buyer will be doing ongoing surveys of prevailing rents for different house types, sizes, features and neighborhoods. They will be looking at whether owners are having to give discounts or incentives to keep their units occupied. If so, they will adjust the rents backwards to come up with a realistic rent in the current market.

You can do the same research, checking rental advertisements in the classifieds and elsewhere. You can also call around as a prospective tenant and get the real story, as sometimes rents are reduced with a prospect on the phone.

There are online resources as well. Doing a Google search on "houses for rent" will give you many sites, from Craigslist.com to Rent.com.

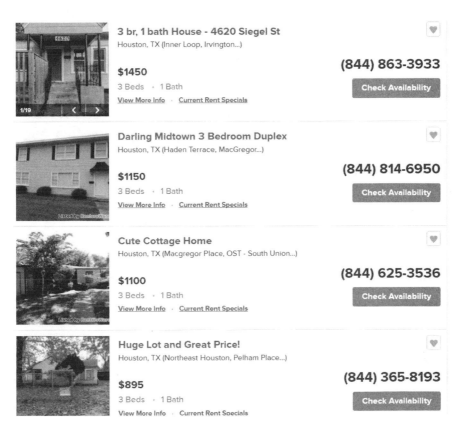

This shot is of a portion of the results for homes for rent with 3 bedrooms in Houston, TX. Zillow.com also lists rentals. Information is there, just gather it, and file it away in the filing system you chose in our previous chapter.

By gaining a knowledge of the range of rents for the type and size of houses in which you're dealing, you can better match up a buyer and a deal.

Cash Flow is King

Once a buyer determines what they can realistically get for rents, they look at their costs, taxes and mortgage to see if that rent range will generate more cash every month than expenses. You should understand this and have some idea of costs. However, the major thing for you to consider is their cost to buy.

If you can sell them a 3 bedroom home at the discount to the market price of smaller homes, then you deliver an advantage to them. They have a 2 bedroom mortgage with a 3 bedroom rent income. They will jump all over deals that give them the cash flow they want.

Value Appreciation

This one is really more of using logic and not dealing in declining neighborhoods. If people are moving away, abandoned foreclosures litter the neighborhood and values are declining, look for deals elsewhere. In more normal markets, appreciation over time is the historical trend.

Market Sold Property Information

Before the next section, we need to cover how you can have the information about homes for sale and sold properties that are used by real estate professionals to sell and value properties.

The local MLS, Multiple Listing Service, is no longer a printed book of listings. It is an online listing database with all the information about listed and sold properties. The power of the online application is that the real estate agents can pull out reports as well as get email updates of new listings and properties sold.

If you're going to search for a local real estate website (this is better than Realtor.com or Zillow.com), put in the search phrase like "yourtown real estate," but add "IDX" to the search.

IDX stands for Internet Data Exchange, and it is an agreement of local MLS members to share their listing data in a way that allows all members to display all listings on their websites. So, when you find one site you like with search features you value, you'll have access to all of the listings of all of the member companies.

In some areas you're even allowed to search for sold properties, but they generally lock that out of their MLS searches. You can however get everything you want simply by asking a local real estate agent to set you up with automated email alerts for new listings, price reductions and sold properties when they close.

It's a one-time 15-minute operation for them and the MLS system does the notifications. Building relationships with real estate professionals is something you should be doing anyway, so you should have no problem finding one or more of them willing to set up automated alerts for you.

You will receive these emails as they happen or once each day, and simply have them go into your chosen note/database system. When you are considering a house for a deal, you can pull up recent sales and current listings in the neighborhood to help you to value the house.

How to Calculate Market Value

Your buyers will know approximately what your house deal is worth in the current market. Some may use real estate agents to help them, but active investors will do what the agents do, a CMA, Comparative Market Analysis.

The CMA is similar to the appraisal, but an appraiser works for the lender and wants to come to a conservative result that protects their lender's investment. A CMA is calculated for sellers to determine the listing price for the home. It is based on market conditions and attempts to get the best price for the seller.

Many of your buyers are using this CMA calculation to determine the value of the home you bring them. The best practice for you is to bring the CMA with you when you present the home. Do it right and be conservative, and you'll be proving your deal's value.

To learn how it works, let's do an example. All of these are just sample numbers, not pulled from any current market, but they are representative of how the process works to show current market value of a house.

The Property

We've found a good deal with a distressed seller with equity. We can sell this ready to rent house to a rental property buyer, so we need to determine its current value on the market. Characteristics:

- 3 BR, 2 BA
- 1250 sq/ft
- Standard subdivision lot
- Two car attached garage
- Standard floor plan in large subdivision with many similar homes

This is the home we're considering as a deal to take to one or more buyers, and we need to see what it is worth on the current market.

The Comps (Comparables)

Comparables are recently sold homes in the same area and comparable to our subject property in size and features. It is best that we find three or more and they should if possible fit these criteria:

- Be similar in bedrooms, baths and size to our subject property.
- Be in the same neighborhood or as nearby a similar neighborhood as possible.
- Sold date should be as near in the past as possible. If it is too old, then the price may not be relevant in today's market.

We find three recent sales in the same subdivision with similar size lots. They all closed within the previous 30 to 90 days. These three are similar to our subject property, but not exactly the same.

Comp A

- 3BR `1.5 BA home
- 1180 sq/ft
- Two car attached garage
- Common floorplan in this subdivision
- Sold price $152,000

Comp B

- 2 BR 2 BA
- 1200 sq/ft
- Single car attached garage
- Commons subdivision floorplan & lot
- Sold price $160,000

Comp C

- 3 BR 2 BA
- 1325 sq/ft
- 2 car attached garage
- Standard subdivision floorplan & lot
- Sold price $174,000

Now that we know our sold prices and house characteristics we must make some adjustments for the differences (to our subject home) in the properties.

Adjustments

We must adjust the sold prices of our comparables to get them closer to what they would have been if the houses had been identical in characteristics to our subject home.

You must think backward here. If the comp home has less in the way of features or smaller (say one fewer baths), then you must ADD to the sold price to make it more like it would have been with the same number of baths. If it's got more in the way of features, such as an extra bedroom, you must SUBTRACT from the sold price.

What we must do is to estimate what the difference is in dollars. We can get the approximate value of a bedroom or a bath from some online websites that have localized information. Or, one good way is to look at almost identical homes that sold and find an example and use the sold price difference.

Example: two identical homes except for one having an extra bedroom had a $14,000 difference in sold prices. So, the approximate value of a bedroom would be $14,000.

Another example: two almost identical houses, but one with only 1.5 baths instead of 2. Difference in sold price was $4,000.

However, this method has no way of knowing the attitudes of sellers and buyers, so it can be off quite a bit. Another and better way is to ask a local appraiser to give you the numbers they use. However you do it, you need to place a value on feature differences.

Comp A

Comp A is almost identical, but it has 1.5 baths instead of 2. A local appraiser tells you that she uses $3,800 in her calculations for this. Other than square footage, which we'll deal with later, this is the only major difference, so we add $3,800 to the sold price of Comp A to get an adjusted sold price of $155,800.

Comp B

This house has one fewer bedrooms and only one garage space. We've determined that the bedroom's value is $12,500 and the single garage space would requirethat we add $7,000 to the price to compensate.. Both of these were shortcomings of this house, so we add these values to its sold price to come up with an adjusted $179,500.

Comp C

We're almost exactly alike with this one except for square footage, so we keep the $174,000 sold price. Now its time to do our calculations to come up with the approximate market value of our subject house. All of the comp sold prices have been adjusted so that in effect they're all exactly alike.

Comp A $155,800 / 1180 sq/ft = $132 per sq/ft

Comp B $160,000 / 1200 sq/ft = 133 per sq/ft

Comp C $174,000 / 1325 sq/ft = $131 per sq ft

First, know that coming this close is really rare, as usually there is more difference than this. However, these are our numbers, so let's finish. Now we average our per square foot prices, which is easy, as it is the middle number, $132 per sq/ft. So, here is the value of our subject home:

$$\$132 \text{ per sq/ft} \times 1250 \text{ sq/ft} = \textbf{\$165,000}$$

This isn't a complicated deal, and we must realize that a lot of these numbers are estimates, but working with the best numbers we have at our disposal, this is the value of our subject home.

Now we know our best buyers would be willing to pay up to a max imum of around $148,500, a 10% discount to current market value.

Bring it All Together

Now that we know what our buyer is willing to pay, what they can rent the home for and their approximate expenses, we know if it's a deal on their side at this price.

Now we simply have to see if we can negotiate a price with the seller that will give us our desired profit to deliver the deal for $148,500 +/-.

Chapter 7

Rehab 101-Understanding Your Buyer Requirements

In the previous chapter you learned what your rental property buyer does to value a property to determine what they're willing to pay for it.

Now, if you were a fix & flip investor, you would need to know that so you can work backward to what you can pay for a house and spend on rehab and still make a profit.

As the snap flipper selling to the fix & flip investor, you need to be able to calculate rehab costs closely enough to work up your deal numbers to leave you and the fix & flip investor a profit when the final buyer takes the property. You will get your money when the fix & flip investor takes over your assignment contract, but you must be able to project his selling price to leave both of you room for your profit.

None of this is a down-to-the-penny process, but you do need to be able to estimate the cost of rehab closely enough to know what the fix & flip investor will need to spend so you can work up your deal for a win-win result. Remember, you and the fix & flip investor are working backward from ARV, After Repair Value, of the home and what a rental buyer will pay for it. An example:

ARV of home you're working a deal on: $146,000

Rental buyer will buy at 10% discount: $131,400

Estimated rehab with financing cost: $18,700

$131,400 - $18,700 = $112,700 breakeven for fix & flip investor

Now we can only guess at what the fix & flip investor wants for a profit, unless we've worked with them before. But, let's just say that they would like to take away around $20,000 from this deal for their work and risk. Now our number is down to $92,700. If we can deliver this house to the fix & flip investor for that amount, we would probably have a deal.

This next part is easier, as we can come up with any reasonable amount we want for our profit. Keeping in mind that we're risking very little and turning the house quickly, we would like to make $10,000 for our efforts.

$82,700 is the magic number for our purchase.

It is obvious that these are all estimates and desired profit numbers, so there is room to do better or worse at every step. However, your snap flip purchase price of $82,700 and profit of $10,000 is the plan. You can negotiate to lock up this house with that goal.

All of that is great, but how do we come up with that $18,700 number for estimated rehab cost? Let's look at some online and other resources to gather estimates of cost for renovation and repairs. You'll find which will work best for you as you gain experience.

Estimating Rehab Costs

Let's look at some of the ways to come to reasonable estimates of rehab costs.

The Human Approach

In this case you can build a relationship with some contractors and home repair companies and get them to give you estimates. This works for fix & flip investors because they can let bids to these people so that they get the work. You don't have that advantage. You can't expect them to keep investing their time and expertise without compensation. Paying for estimates isn't something you want to do either.

One way around this is knowing who your most active fix & flip investors use for contractors and getting them to estimate the work. Then you can not only deliver the deal but the estimate as well. This way the contractors have a reasonable expectation of getting some work and compensation for their estimates.

The drawback of the human approach if you can make it work is the time factor. Great deals usually will not sit around and wait for long.

Online & Software Estimation Tools

Some of these are downloadable spreadsheets, but most are done online. One thing to remember is that these are set up for consumer homeowners. So, the estimates are for contractors they may hire, like a retail project.

You are working more toward the wholesale end, meaning what the cost would be for the contractor rather than after it is marked up for the retail customer. They can still be useful, but you would discount the result by an arbitrary percentage.

RemodelingCalculator.org

This site provides an online calculator with various rooms and projects. It's pretty quick and you can even select the quality range; low end, midrange or high end. One approach could be to choose low end and use that as your more wholesale oriented number. It also adjusts for your geographical area.

Calculate Remodel Costs Now!

Select Project	Bathroom ▾
Bath/Shower Type	Shower ▾
Bathroom Details	✔ Toilet, Sink, Lights
	✔ Plumbing
	✔ Tile Floors
	☐ Tile on Walls
Project Size	140 sq. ft.
Materials Quality	Basic ▾
Project Type	New Construction ▾
US Region	National Average ▾

Estimate Cost

Low End	Mid Range	High End
$0	$0	$0

See costs in your area
Start Here - Enter Your Zip Code   Enter ZIP   **GET LOCAL PRICES**

BuildingAdvisor.com

This site allows you to download a detailed and free estimation spreadsheet, much like the one the contractors use. It is more detailed than you may want, but you can generalize and use what you want and leave the rest alone.

Estimating & Budgeting Spreadsheet

View all ESTIMATING articles

Learn about our new *PREMIUM ESTIMATING SPREADSHEET*. Try Risk-Free today with this *SPECIAL OFFER*.

The **BuildingAdvisor Estimating & Budgeting Spreadsheet** is available free as an Excel spreadsheet (.xls) and a Word document (.doc). The construction estimating spreadsheet includes formulas to track cost estimates, actual costs, variances, payments, and balances due. Most builders prefer spreadsheets over more complicated estimating software. You can use the BuildingAdvisor spreadsheet to estimate and track costs for both building and remodeling projects. Uses include:

- **Checklist for budgeting: Make sure all important items on the list are accounted for in your preliminary budget**

- **Checklist for estimating: Make sure all items get into your detailed estimate**

- **Tracking estimated vs. actual costs for each line item (called "job costing")**

- **Tracking payments and amount due to all vendors and subcontractors**

Download Free ESTIMATING WORKSHEET (.xls) **to use with Excel to calculate costs and track expenses.**

Download free ESTIMATING WORKSHEET (.doc) **for a printable "read-only" estimating worksheet.**

View Sample of The Estimating Spreadsheet Below:

HomeRenovationEstimate.com

This site is another consumer oriented online calculation tool. There are many others if you do a Google search on "home renovation estimate." Here is what the home page of this site looks like:

Estimate Calculators

Roof Renovation and Roof Repair

Sloped Roofs — Estimate Costs

Flat Roofs — Estimate Costs

Exterior Wall Siding — Estimate Costs
alluminium, stucco & more..

Eavestroughs — Estimate Costs

Deck Construction — Estimate Costs

Patio Construction — Estimate Costs

Fence Construction — Estimate Costs

Driveways and Walkways — Estimate Costs

Landscaping — Estimate Costs

Garage Renovations — Estimate Costs

Windows : — Estimate Costs
Replacements and Window Installation

Exterior Doors — Estimate Costs
Installation and Build

Stairs and Railing Renovations — Estimate Costs

Bathroom : — Estimate Costs
Renovation and Bathroom Remodeling

Kitchen : — Estimate Costs

WELCOME to Home Renovation Estimat

Calculate your Home Renovation Costs Online

Our easy to use home renovation cost calculators allow you to get project cost estimates online. Home Renovation Estimate – provides the most sophisticated online home renovation cost calculator and is totally free. Simply choose a project from the navigation menu on the left and get your home renovation estimate free online.

»

Featured services

In addition to our fully functioning online home renovation cost calculator, we offer a free contractor and professional service directory. Also available is free information for home owners and contractors in our Home Renovation Estimate Blog. The home Renovation Estimate website is complete free to use.

»

Free Home Renovation Estimate Newsletter

Get interesting articles, news, and information directly to your email FREE! Simply sign up and start receiving our home renovation newsletters. Your email address will not be sold, given away or used for any other purpose. Opt out at any time easily.

Name [   ]   Email [   ]

SUBMIT »

Don't Get Bogged Down in Detail

We are talking about snap flipping, so it seems to go against the concept if you have to spend hours or even days doing detailed estimates of rehab costs. Sure, you need to come up with some idea, as you want your fix & flip buyer to take the house with a profit in it for you and them.

The good news is that as you get better and more experienced, you'll get faster at coming up with reasonable estimates that let you put together a deal. There is also the swag method. As you get experienced, you can over-estimate with high conservative numbers. When you offer the home to your fix & flip investor, they may turn you down, but you then have some room to negotiate.

The better news is that you have little or none of your money tied up (we'll show you later), so if they don't take it, you can simply let your assignment contract expire without taking any action.

The best way to protect yourself and your deal is to negotiate the lowest possible price for the house. This leaves you room to adjust your profit within your limits to make the deal work.

Your Buyers Will Buy if You Meet their Needs

Working with these numbers and getting your purchase price right should give you high confidence in selling the deal to an investor buyer on your list at a profit. The more buyers you have and the better you get at your business, the more often you'll have more than one buyer wanting the property. There's nothing wrong with a little competition!

Chapter 8

Introduction to the Math of Investing

Don't start pulling your hair out or thinking, if I have to learn all of this, instead I'll just get a job at Walmart. First, you don't have to learn or memorize anything here. Second, it's really simple stuff, and the more of it you understand the better you're likely to do in your business.

You can even skip this chapter now and use it as a reference when you get to your first potential deal and wonder how your investor buyer is going to evaluate it. We already covered the CMA, Comparative Market Analysis, to come to ARV, After Repair Value in the current market.

One way to think about this chapter and these calculations is as a stepping stone to even bigger deals and larger profits. Some of these calculations are used mostly in commercial real estate and multi-family investing in apartments. Don't limit your thinking, as you may want to plow some of your snap flipping profits into other real estate investments as your business grows.

GPI – Gross Potential Income

This calculation is used mostly in multi-family investment, but it applies in single family homes as rental properties as well.

GPI is the expected income from a rental property or properties if they are fully rented and all rents are paid on time and in full. For your deal purposes, what will the end rental property investor get for income in a perfect world.

It will be the amount of the rent multiplied by 12 months in the year. Let's use a rental example, a house renting for $1.200/month.

$$GPI = Monthly\ Rent\ \$ \times 12\ months$$

$$GPI = \$1,200 \times 12 = \$14,400$$

We're assuming the home will be rented for 365 days of the year and the tenant will always pay their rent. Of course, this is almost a perfect world, but it happens. For the snap flipper, you may be talking with a buyer who uses this term and you want to know what they're talking about.

GOI – Gross Operating Income

There are two top level expense items with rental homes:

1. Vacancy loss
2. Credit loss

When the tenant leaves, there is an unknown amount of time that the unit will be unoccupied and rent will not be collected. This is called Vacancy Loss. Until a new tenant is in place, the lost rent is this expense.

Credit loss is when the tenant is in the property but they miss some rent, give you a bad check; in other words they don't pay in full.

An active rental property investor who has owned properties for a while will have past history numbers for these two items. They are normally expressed as a percentage.

If there is no history to estimate these expense items, an estimated percentage is used. If the rental investor finds that similar properties and information that can be found shows 6% on average for Vacancy and Credit Loss, then that number can be used in budgeting.

For you, the snap flipper, this is just good information. It is good to know that your rent research showing $1,200 for current rents for this size home will not be the number used by the end rental property investor. They will see their GOI, using our previous example, to be:

$$GOI = GPI - Vacancy \ \& \ Credit \ Loss$$

$$GOI = \$14,400 - (\$14,400 \ X \ .06)$$

$$GOI = \$14,400 - \$864 = \$13,536$$

These by far aren't the only expenses, but they are normally considered off the top in this way before considering other operational expenses. Let's do that next.

NOI – Net Operating Income

The NOI, Net Operating Income is what is left in the bank after the expenses. This is NOT cash flow unless the property is owned free and clear. The mortgage payments are not considered in this calculation because we don't know if there is a mortgage. Also, to compare properties, this allows an apples-to-apples comparison of the performance of two properties whether mortgaged or not.

This calculation includes expenses for management, legal and accounting, insurance, janitorial, maintenance, supplies, taxes, utilities, etc. Using a spreadsheet, the rental investor would enter all of these individual expenses and total them up as an annual amount. For our running example, lets use these numbers:

Real estate taxes = $1,100

Maintenance = $225

Supplies = $120

Utilities (water/sewer) = $360

Legal & Accounting = $320

Advertising = $85

Total expenses = $2,210

NOI = GOI – Total Annual Expenses

NOI = $13,536 - $2,210 = $11,326

Now you can appreciate the end rental investor buyer's negotiation position. They are working with a net number, and they are also probably paying a mortgage payment. They know what they can pay for a home and get some positive cash flow. Anything over that will not result in a purchase.

This runs back up the chain, as the fix & flip investor must be able to deliver a property to fit this investor's requirements. You must deliver a property that allows the fix & flip investor to do that and still make a profit for themselves.

Cap Rate – Capitalization Rate

This is one used mostly by commercial and multi-family investors, but you want to appear to be savvy when you hear it mentioned, and you may expand and need it down the road.

The Cap Rate is a number used to compare properties and calculate value or selling price in the current market. Our ongoing example property has been assigned no value at this point, so let's say that the current value or the price we paid is $180,000. The Cap Rate is the Net Operating Income divided by the value or price.

$$CAP\ Rate = NOI\ /\ Value\text{-}Price$$

$$CAP\ Rate = \$11,326\ /\ \$180,000$$

$$CAP\ Rate = .063\ or\ 6.3\%$$

Investors use this to compare properties. The reason is that the NOI of a property can be very different based simply on how well the owner controls expenses, or on how low taxes may be, etc. Two almost identical properties with the same rent could have very different Cap Rates simply because one has much lower expenses.

If an investor is considering buying one of the two, they could use the Cap Rates as an initial indicator to look more deeply into the operations to find out where the difference is.

More But Not for Snap Flipping

There are other financial calculations for evaluating real estate investments, but they really aren't what you need to snap flip. These should give you the expertise you need to hold your own when a buyer is trying to find out if you know what you're talking about when you say you can deliver good investment properties.

Chapter 9

Finding Properties Before the Competition

You have enough information now to evaluate potential houses that could be profitable snap flip deals. However, how do you locate them to do your evaluations? We know what makes a home stand out of the crowd, but we need to narrow down that crowd and zero in on the best of them.

The snap flipper's value in the transaction is delivering deals that their buyer(s) do not have the time to locate, can't locate, or simply do not want to bother. There are buyers out there who prefer that a good snap flipper with talent do the legwork and preliminary valuation and serve up the deals on a silver platter.

We love snap flippers and eagerly look at the deals the good ones deliver to us. We buy a significant number of our rental properties from snap flippers who know how to do their job and do not waste our time delivering poor deals.

The key to your success is to set up systems to locate as many potential deals as possible. You need to cull through hundreds of potential deal candidates to zero in on a few that you can work into deals.

You will find some of these resources quite useful, some not so much. Some will be too time consuming for you, especially if you get some great online resources set up that you can check daily or have alerts sent to you.

Your goal is to use the resources that bring as many potential deals to your attention as possible, and hopefully even provide enough information, financial and condition, to help you to weed the bad ones out quickly.

We'll start with traditional resources like the classifieds, etc. Then let's look at the harnessing the power of the Internet and searches.

Classifieds

Yes, the classifieds are old school, but they still work or there wouldn't be pages of them in the newspapers. They are cheap to run, so some homeowners in distress will run "must sell" type ads here. Checking them out every morning could give you a head start on a good deal.

You can also run your own ads to try and get distressed owners to call you. Advertise that you buy homes for cash in a hurry, or that you help homeowners sell to avoid foreclosure.

Craigslist

This is a search on Craigslist in a city for "must sell by owner." Here you get the advantages of classifieds for free and the ability to search for what you want with keywords to zero in faster.

You can also run ads here to attract distressed sellers. They may be trying to avoid foreclosure or they need to sell in a hurry to relocate for a job.

One snap flipper found a niche in locating tired landlords with properties they have allowed to deteriorate in condition with the rents dropping accordingly. They are fix & flip candidates and usually without mortgages. Finding those can make for quick deals, as the owners just want out from under them and the headaches of being landlords.

Foreclosure Websites

We've touched on these before, but let's go through them again from the perspective of locating the gems that you can snap flip for profit.

Realtytrac.com

◉ AUCTION (FORECLOSURE SALE) Raines St Scranton, PA 18509	**$59,131** (Est. Opening Bid) Auction Date: 12/15/2016

◉ AUCTION (FORECLOSURE SALE) Greenbush St Scranton, PA 18508	**$81,558** (Est. Opening Bid) Auction Date: 12/15/2016

◉ AUCTION (FORECLOSURE SALE) S Hyde Park Ave Scranton, PA 18504	**$277,118** (Est. Opening Bid) Auction Date: 12/15/2016

◉ AUCTION (FORECLOSURE SALE) Saint Ann St Scranton, PA 18504	**$111,909** (Est. Opening Bid) Auction Date: 12/15/2016

◉ AUCTION (FORECLOSURE SALE) S Irving Ave Scranton, PA 18505	**$80,663** (Est. Opening Bid) Auction Date: 12/15/2016

◉ AUCTION (FORECLOSURE SALE) N Garfield Ave Scranton, PA 18504	**$105,130** (Est. Opening Bid) Auction Date: 12/15/2016

These are auction listings on the site. There are also foreclosure and pre-foreclosure listings. The pre-foreclosure and auction listings are often better resources. You're not going to the auction to bid, as you don't want to win a house and have to put up cash right away to buy it.

You check out the auctions to see which properties end up being bought by the lender to become bank owned properties. This means no other investors were interested enough to bid high enough to get them.

However, now you know which are about to become listed foreclosure properties and you have some time to do a little due diligence to see which you may want to watch to buy when the price is right.

Sheriffsales.net

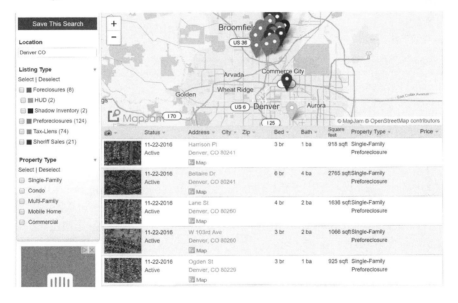

This site lists nationwide pre-foreclosure and sheriff sales of real estate. It even allows you to set up email alerts for new listings as they appear.

Fannie Mae Homepath

Fannie Mae is one of the two largest quasi-government entities that guarantee most of the home mortgages. When Fannie Mae takes back a property they want to sell it and get it off the books. You can search their site for their foreclosures.

This site and the others like it are sources for leads for you. Buying these properties isn't usually what you are trying to do. The banks/lenders will not allow our primary purchase method, the assignment contract, in most cases. There is a way to buy foreclosures that we'll talk about later. However, to fully employ the advantages of snap flipping, you don't want to actually buy anything if possible.

Good Old Fashioned Legwork

Some of the best deals you'll find with the greatest profit potential will not be found on the Web or in advertising. They will be found by networking, driving around and tips from others.

Abandoned Homes & Service Providers

Sometimes homeowners just abandon their homes. They need to move for work, can't sell for whatever reason, so they just pick up and move. They are probably going to be in foreclosure soon, but they often leave before the formal process begins.

Finding these homes before any formal foreclosure processes begin and before there is any public notice gives you an advantage. Cultivating friendships with vendors and others who are often the first to know about abandoned homes is a good way to learn about them:

- Meter readers
- Electric company people who pull meters for non-payment
- Gas company employees who turn off gas for non-payment
- Newspaper carriers who see papers piling up
- Homeowner associations who see grass growing tall against association rules
- Homeowner associations who stop getting monthly or quarterly homeowner dues

Virtually anyone who is out and about and observant could clue you into a home that seems recently abandoned.

Drive Around & Learn Your Market Area

Spend spare time out and about in your market area. Get used to the look and activity in neighborhoods. The next time you pass through you may just see something unusual to clue you that a home is a prospect.

No matter how you find out about an abandoned property, you can take the address to the courthouse and look up the address where the tax bill is mailed. If a mortgage is recorded, you can also see what is owed on the property.

If it could be a prospect for a deal, you can send a letter to the tax address offering to help them to sell and asking them to contact you.

Business Cards

Let everyone you know that your business is helping owners to sell their homes when they haven't been able to do so or they need cash in a hurry.

Hand out business cards to everyone. You never know when someone will call to tell you that they have a friend who is in trouble and needs to sell. You're first in line in this case and it could be your next deal.

Chapter 10

Ninja Foreclosure Tactics

Shed no tears for America's banks and mortgage lenders. Almost all the mortgages they issue have some type of government guarantees to get back some of their investment in the event of a default.

However, that's when the lender holds and services the mortgage. Many mortgages are packaged up and sold to Fannie Mae and Freddie Mac, taking the lender totally off the hook in the event of default. The lenders don't wait 30 years to collect interest. They sell the loan and pocket some profits within months or shorter of issuing it.

Once a mortgage is foreclosed, it is auctioned, but usually ends up purchased back by the lender. Fannie Mae and Freddie Mac handle most of their own foreclosures, listing them on their websites and with real estate brokerages.

Some foreclosures are placed into the hands of asset management companies, not even part of the lender's staff. They are specialists at handling foreclosures and getting them sold as quickly as possible for the best price possible.

Notice that there is a pattern here. When you decide to make an offer on a foreclosure home, you're not handing that offer to somebody's uncle or mother over the kitchen table. You don't have to look at their faces or face their wrath when you make the necessary lowball offer that will make your deal work.

You're dealing with a faceless entity. Even if you're giving your offer to a real estate agent, they're simply forwarding it as-is to a faceless entity. In fact, Fannie Mae has mandated online offers. So, even if there is a listing agent, a form with only the information they want will be used to make an offer.

12822 Huntington Venture Dr Houston, Texas 77099
Updated: Nov 23, 2016 12:14:03 AM ET

$163,000

Status: Price Reduced

Single Family   ♥ Save Listing

4 Beds | 4 Baths | 2,690 sq. ft.

REO ID: D1600V2

MLS ID: 10145774

Make an Offer   How to make an offer

You can even register with Fannie Mae HomePath to make offers directly as an individual.

PURCHASE OFFER NO:

OMB Control No. 2900-0029
Respondent Burden: 20 Minutes
Expiration Date: 10/31/2017

VA Department of Veterans Affairs	OFFER TO PURCHASE AND CONTRACT OF SALE

Privacy Act Notice: VA and the Service Provider will not disclose information collected on this form to any source other than what has been authorized under the Privacy Act of 1974 or Title 38, Code of Federal Regulations 1.576 for routine uses (i.e., The information collected on this form will serve as an offer to purchase a VA-acquired property. The acquisition and sale of such property is authorized by law (38 U.S.C. 3720 (a) (5)).) as identified in the VA system of records, 55VA26, Loan Guaranty Home, Condominium and Manufactured Home Loan Applicant Records, Specially Adapted Housing Applicant Records and Vendee Loan Applicant Records - VA, and published in the Federal Register. Your obligation to respond is required to obtain or retain benefits.

Respondent Burden: We need this information to consider your offer to purchase a VA acquired property. Title 38, United States Code, allows us to ask for this information. We estimate that you will need an average of 20 minutes to review the instructions, find the information, and complete this form. VA and the Service Provider cannot conduct or sponsor a collection of information unless a valid OMB control number is displayed. You are not required to respond to a collection of information if this number is not displayed. Valid OMB control numbers can be located on the OMB Internet Page at www.reginfo.gov/public/do/PRAMain. If desired, you can call 1-800-827-1000 to get information on where to send comments or suggestions about this form.

INSTRUCTIONS TO BROKER - Follow the instructions of the Service Provider to submit offer.

1A. ADDRESS OF PROPERTY TO BE PURCHASED *(Include No., Street or rural route, City or P.O. Box, State and ZIP Code)*	1B. PROPERTY IDENTIFIER

SECTION I - PURCHASER(S) INFORMATION			
2A. NAME OF PURCHASER	2B. ADDRESS OF PURCHASER *(Include No., Street or rural route, City or P.O. Box, State and ZIP Code)*	2C. HOME PHONE	
		2D. BUSINESS PHONE	
3A. NAME OF PURCHASER	3B. ADDRESS OF PURCHASER *(Include No., Street or rural route, City or P.O. Box, State and ZIP Code) (If same as above write "SAME")*	3C. HOME PHONE	
		3D. BUSINESS PHONE	

The Veterans Administration has an online PDF form for making offers. You can see the process is becoming automated and tech-oriented.

The point that's really important here is that you're not sitting across a table negotiating. You don't have to look at the other party, the seller. There is no emotion on their side and should be none on yours. This is a business negotiation, and you should know what you can pay and not pay a dollar more.

It's More Fun When You Can Play Hard Ball

Not having to worry about offending the seller with a very low offer and getting told to take a hike makes it more fun to negotiate foreclosures. In most cases, the snap flipper will need to get a property for no more than around 60% of its current as-is value anyway. So, starting with a 40% of list offer is a working strategy.

Yes, if it's on the market as-is for $120,000 and needing a lot of work, offering around $50,000 is a viable strategy. Will you get an excited call from the listing agent or the seller thanking you for taking it off their hands at that price quickly? NOT A CHANCE.

What you will get is either no response till the offer expires or a rejection of your offer. In neither of these cases will you be told to move to the Arctic because they don't want to see your name on an offer ever again. They simply move on and so should you; which brings us to the ninja strategy.

Pick the properties nobody else seems to want.

When a foreclosure first comes on the market, you can certainly make that very low offer, but it's usually wasted time and effort. When you have an interest in a property, monitor the listing, go see it, take photos, start thinking about the rehab budget, etc.

If it gets sold right away, then you would have had to pay too much to work a viable deal anyway. You're watching the properties that just sit there. You're getting email alerts if possible that tell you when a price reduction is posted.

You could be watching 20 or 30 homes at a time, but it's simply watching and waiting until the reduced price approaches a number you think will work with your offer. You have your number calculated, and you simply watch the price reduction activity. Let's do a fictional example to see how it works.

Example Foreclosure Listing

A foreclosed home hits the market at $130,000. It is going to need significant repairs and rehab, so no rental investors want it. The fix & flip investors may have easier pickings, so either they bid low or nobody offers. You set up your alert watch for price reductions. You've also determined that you can make a profitable deal if you can get it for $60,000.

In three weeks, the price is reduced to $115,000. You take note but you wait longer. In another month, the price is reduced to $99,000. You make a $60,000 offer. They ignore it or reject it. The reason you go to your real number now is that the longer it stays on the market and has more price reductions, the greater the risk you will lose it. So, make your top offer now to grab it quickly. They ignore or reject it.

However, you keep waiting and they lower it again to $89,000. You come back with an offer of $50,000. They see you have offered before and your offer has gone down. They're obviously wanting it sold, so they may take your offer. Instead, they reject it.

They drop the price again to $79,000, and you make an offer of

$40,000. They see your strategy now, so they decide to try to work it out. You get a counter offer of $69,000. You just keep working them down until they reach your $60,000 target or lower if you can pull it off.

The beauty of this strategy is that you're investing a little time and calculating and then just sitting back and waiting for your opportunities to come to you. Is there a risk you'll never get a property? Sure, but if that's what is happening, you may need to readjust your calculations and assume you can pay a little more because you can get a little more in the current competitive environment.

Pre-Foreclosure Strategies

You can use a different approach by watching pre-foreclosures. If you find that you have strong and active rental property buyers, you can watch the pre-foreclosures for jewels that your buyers would love to buy.

These would be ready-to-rent, no repairs necessary, homes in desirable neighborhoods. These homes are not foreclosed yet, and you may have the time to make an offer directly to the owner to get it before it goes to auction. If so, you can often make a great deal just because you're swooping in at the last moment to save them from foreclosure.

Of course, the numbers have to work. And, you'll want to have a buyer or two lined up for a very fast transfer. It may be that the numbers don't work due to the mortgage debt. However, you may be able to do a short sale offer. Nationally, lenders are averaging more than $30,000 in costs to foreclose and go to market. You will save them that money and it just may get your offer accepted.

The worst case is that you wait for it to foreclose and go into your ninja strategy and watch it.

About Short Sales

A short sale is when you make an offer to the lender with a selling price below the balance on the mortgage. In other words, if accepted, they're settling for a price short of what they're owed.

However, to avoid the costs and time involved in foreclosure, they may just take your offer.

The Process

It isn't a simple process, but you may find it worth the effort to grab properties before the competition even gets notice of their availability. You are working with the homeowner who is behind on their mortgage.

You must get the homeowner to work with you and give written permission to the lender for you to negotiate on their behalf. The owners will not care, as it's this or foreclosure. However, you must gather personal information and get their active help in making this happen.

In many cases, short sale offers come before the lender is even certain that a foreclosure will be necessary. The borrower is behind, but the lender may be expecting some attempt to modify the loan or efforts to pay payments up to a point just short of foreclosure.

What you must do is to help the homeowner to create a "hardship letter." This is submitted with your offer. You have them gather all their debts, payments, medical expenses, layoff notices or anything that shows they are unable to pay their payments in the future. In other words, foreclosure is imminent.

Itemize their expenses, debts and financial problems to show the lender that there is no hope for the borrower to catch up their payments or avoid foreclosure. This prepares the lender for the looming foreclosure expenses to come.

Now you get to do one of those CMAs, Comparative Market Analysis, you learned about earlier. You want to show the lender that there is little or no chance of them getting any more than your offer for the home. Or, at the very least, they will not get enough more to pay the costs of the foreclosure process.

The comparable properties, comps, you select in this case are not regular retail sales. Instead you seek out comparable homes that sold in foreclosure or at auction. This is a more accurate depiction of what the lender can expect if they go forward with the foreclosure.

Now you're ready to make your offer and include these two attachments:

1. Hardship letter
2. CMA for market value

It's impossible to know if the lender will respond or counter your offer. You're not in the same situation as the foreclosure, so too deep of a discount to the amount owed probably will not work. However, if you have a convincing CMA and it validates your offer, you just may have a deal.

These strategies are dealing with lenders or asset managers. They are unlikely to consider assignment offers. Later you'll learn about transaction funding which will allow you to make offers you can fund.

Chapter 11

Negotiation with Owner Sellers

We've talked about this in the chapter on your role in this snap flipping business. However, it is critical that you understand the motivations of owner sellers and your role in helping them to achieve their goal.

There are two types of deals that will make up most of your business.

1. Sale of a home in need of rehab to a fix & flip investor.

2. Sale of a home that's in good condition to a rental property investor.

Owner Sellers & the Rental Property Buyer

This will be a house that may need cosmetic or minor repairs, but nothing rising to the level of a major repair or rehab project. This is because your best rental property buyer is one who doesn't want to have to do much or delay long before installing a renter and generating cash flow.

Many rental buyers are buying from the fix & flip investor, as they are specializing in making a rough property ready to rent just for this buyer type. The good news is that you're also going to be selling to their fix & flip supplier as well. However, for this section, the house will be in a condition that makes it ready to rent with little or no work.

Since many of today's available foreclosures have been sitting vacant for a while, they are mostly going to fall into the category of needing rehab. For this reason, to supply your rental buyers, you will often be dealing with an owner occupant or out of area owner.

The Owner Seller's Situation

Because you're going to need to sell to the rental property buyer at some discount to current market value and make a profit, you will not be dealing with buyers who want or must get close to full retail value for their homes.

Your typical owner seller will be in some situation of distress in their financial lives. They must sell their homes, and the extent of their distress and the equity they have in their homes will determine if you can make a deal or not. Their situations vary, but often include:

- Need to move in a hurry for a better job.
- Medical bills make affording the mortgage payment impossible.
- In default or about to default on mortgage and they want to avoid a foreclosure.
- Need to sell but do not have enough equity to afford real estate commissions and still pay off mortgage; can't bring cash to the closing table.

Those are the primary situations you'll encounter. They are living in the home, so many will be in ready to rent condition or close to it. They may be contacting you from your marketing, bandit signs, ads, Craigslist or other. Or, you may find them from networking and a tip. However you locate a distressed owner wanting to sell, the right approach is critical to making a deal.

First, is it even a possible deal?

We're talking about a rental buyer and a home that is in good condition. The first step is to do a CMA, Comparative Market Analysis, to determine the current market value of the home. This gives you half of the possible deal calculation.

Second, you must get some information from the seller about the home and liens on it. What is their first mortgage balance? Are there any second mortgages and if so what are their balances? You'll also need to know about any tax or mechanics liens that they know about. This gives you what you need for the viability calculation:

Market Value – Owed on Home = $ to work with

If the market value minus all owed on the home is a tiny number or a negative number, it's almost always going to be a deal you can't make. The only situation where this can work is if it is a great home in a high demand neighborhood and you think it is worth the time and effort to try and do a short sale transaction.

However, if there is some equity, particularly if there is enough to make your profit and satisfy your rental buyer's price cut, then you may have a deal. This is where you can hit a brick wall if the seller expects to walk away with their equity. Obviously, there is no deal if the selling price minus the debt isn't enough for you to profit.

Seller Situation & Frank Conversation

We've already discussed the fact that your role is one of a business person who must make a profit. However, you are also a life preserver for a drowning homeowner. They are often in denial. They contact you off an ad that says you buy houses fast for cash. They want that, but the problem is that they don't understand your business model and the fact that much if not all of their equity is going to be sacrificed if they want to get out from under the home.

It is perfectly OK, actually beneficial, to explain your business first. Tell them what you do. Letting them understand that you have buyers ready to pay cash for their home, but they have their own investment criteria. You must meet those criteria and leave some room for your business to profit from your efforts on their behalf.

Level of Distress versus Equity Forfeit

This is when you discuss their situation with them and determine how badly they really NEED to sell and how quickly. Before you got to their kitchen table, they must already have found that the normal real estate agent listing process wasn't going to work for them.

If the bread winner has lost their job, mortgage payments are no longer possible, and a new job is waiting in a new area, they probably are motivated enough to just want to get out from under the home quickly. The equity they may have is secondary to losing the new job or moving and leaving the home for foreclosure.

You are not there to rub it in. You empathize with their situation, but you can't sympathize. Lay out the numbers for them and give them your purchase offer number. Be prepared for some shock, but it will be less if you have had the recommended discussions with them about what you do.

If there is any room for negotiation on price, make the offer that leaves you that room. If they ask if you can do better, then you can say that you'll check with your buyers and see if you can free up some negotiation room. Take a day, get back with them, and come to your top price.

You ARE NOT taking advantage of their situation. It is an opportunity for you, but you are delivering a solution to the biggest problem in their financial lives now.

Your relationship with these sellers and the number of deals you'll get done will depend a lot on your ability to be empathetic with a sincere desire to help them. Balanced with their understanding of what you do and your need for profit, you'll be successful more often than not if the numbers work. Remember, you are not disclosing the price your buyer will be paying.

Owner Sellers and the Fix & Flip Buyer

The fix & flip buyer is buying a home in poor to rough condition. They are making money both on the improvement value but also on their rehab work. However, this means that you are working on a two-level deal structure.

They must buy low enough to do the rehab and profit from it when selling at a discount to a rental buyer in most cases. The sellers you'll locate with homes that fit the bill are likely to be:

- Tired landlords with deferred maintenance properties, but usually mortgage free.
- Owners who have abandoned their homes and left them in poor condition or the homes have suffered from vandalism.
- Older homeowners who have a lot of deferred maintenance, but they also have a mortgage free home or a very low mortgage balance.
- Estate managers trying to sell a rough property.

Some of these prospects will come from your marketing. Others will come from keeping up with obituaries and a lot of courthouse research. Watching pre-foreclosures to find offer opportunities may be helpful as well, however the mortgage balances may make waiting for the foreclosure to happen and dealing with the lender a better approach.

Different Motivations

These sellers are often not in a situation where they are trying to avoid foreclosure. They own the property free and clear, but they've let it deteriorate in condition. Now it's going to require a lot of work to try and sell it on the retail market. They normally would just rather get rid of it and take some money away from the closing table.

By the time you've located most of these owners, you've done your ARV, After Repair Value, calculation. You also know about what the ultimate rental buyer will be able to rent the property for. With this information, you've decided on a price you can pay to work for your profit and the fix & flip buyer.

When you get in touch with the owner, you can make your offer, and if they own free and clear, you'll know about what they're going to take away at closing. Make a somewhat lower offer, as they'll likely want to negotiate.

The estate manager will have a goal of getting the property sold to pay off estate debts and give the balance to heirs. If you hit a number they can sell to the heirs, you'll get your deal. Always with offers for these houses, give the seller a rough breakdown of what's going to be required in rehab costs to make the property sellable in the current market.

Negotiating with owners rather than banks and lenders requires more skill and some empathy. However, it can be a niche with less competition and one where your skill at locating properties can make you a lot of money.

Chapter 12

Funding with an Assignment Contract

Now we're getting to the HOW of the snap flip when it comes to funding it and getting that profit with little or no cash from your pocket. This is where the rubber meets the road as they say.

The absolute beauty of our snap flipping process is that this crucial funding piece is really quite simple. Before we get into the detail, lets take a moment to go over how we got here and why we've decided to use an assignment contract.

Where We Are

You have been using the techniques in this book and in what you have learned from us in our seminars and courses to build out a nice list of buyers, both fix & flip and rental property investors.

You have the criteria of your buyers in mind when you go out and use the marketing and networking strategies we teach to locate potential properties matching their criteria.

After doing the due diligence and running the numbers, you found that if you could get the home for the right price, you would have at least one buyer ready to take it off your hands quickly.

You've negotiated with a distressed seller. You aren't working with a foreclosure because it is rare that a lender or asset manager will accept an assignment contract. Your seller has indicated they will accept your offer. Now, what's next?

The Purchase Contract

Real estate transactions are regulated by the states. Generally there are resources for state mandated or approved real estate purchase contracts. Though they are copyrighted, some investors use the same forms Realtors use. However, there are sources for state specific real estate contracts.

This is one of several online resources for these purchase agreements. Though they say these are legal in every respect by state, your best bet is to pass one by a real estate attorney or even have them provide you with one to protect your interests.

The first thing you need to do is to read the contract form you intend to use. If there are any clauses in it that would forbid the use of an assignment or restrict your ability to assign the contract in any way and to anyone you choose, just strike them out.

Changes and Additions to the Purchase Contract

The most basic change is in the place where you fill in the name of the buyer. If you were buying this property, it would be Your Name. Since you're assigning the deal to another, you would simply add a little text: "BUYER: Your Name and/or assigns." This indicates that you may assign the contract to someone else.

Assignment of a contract transfers your rights under the contract. In other words, whatever the terms of the contract, including price, you will transfer to the buyer your rights as to that price and the seller performing as the contract specifies.

However, that's only half of it. The assignment will also transfer your OBLIGATIONS under the contract. This means that for all practical purposes, you no longer have any involvement or requirement to perform under the contract. All of that passes to your buyer as well.

This isn't legal advice, and we have some contract samples to share in our snap flipping training. However, some clauses to help cover your interests could include:

"Upon default, seller's sole and only remedy shall be to retain buyer's earnest money." AND:

"This contract is contingent upon the Buyer's inspection and approval of subject property prior to transfer of title. The seller agrees to provide access to the subject property to the Buyer's representatives, with power and utilities on, prior to transfer of title. If accepted, property will convey in "AS IS" condition. If not accepted, Buyer will notify Seller by phone and in writing within 10 days from the date of this contract."

Presenting and Explaining the Contract

If you're following our process, you've probably already explained that you take homes to qualified investor buyers, now you just explain that the assignment is how you do that.

You tell them that these changes to the standard purchase agreement simply allow you to pass the deal on to your cash buyer who will take over and close the purchase within the contractual time frame.

At this point you negotiate earnest money. This is the smallest amount you can get away with providing at the signing of the assignment contract. It indicates your intent to get the deal done. You're trying to get this down as low as you can, hopefully between $100 and $500 tops.

Your earnest money is only at risk until you and your buyer execute the assignment agreement we'll talk about next. At that time your requirement is that your buyer give you the amount of your earnest money. It's coming back to them anyway, as it is part of the escrow amount applied to the purchase price.

The Assignment Contract with Your Buyer

You're halfway there. Now all you have to do is to take your property workup, you know, the CMA value estimate (ARV, After Repair Value) and your contract to your investor buyer(s).

One lucky buyer will be assigned your rights and obligations in your purchase agreement using an assignment contract form.

Here are the necessary elements of this assignment contract:

- It should clearly show the property address and/or legal description.
- A clause stating that the Assignor (you) is making no representations as to the purchase contract or the condition of the property. All due diligence is the responsibility of the Assignee (your buyer).
- A "Hold Harmless" clause stating that the Assignee agrees to hold the Assignor harmless and indemnify the Assignor against any claims or damages related to the contract or the transaction.
- A clear statement that the Assignee accepts the rights and

the obligations of the Assignor under the contract, dated and time. This sets out the time of the transfer of rights and obligations.

- A clause that sets out the reimbursement of your earnest money deposit. You want to get this money at the time of assignment, as should the deal fall through, you at least do not want to lose that deposit.

- Terms for the payment of your fee. In some rare cases you may be able to get some or all of it at the time of assignment, but usually it is to be paid at closing.

Once your assignment contract is signed by both parties and you collect your earnest money, you just sit back and wait for closing to get your nice fat check. Now you need only notify the seller that you have assigned the contract and who they will be dealing with in the future as the buyer.

What Can Go Wrong?

If you're working with an experienced and active investor buyer, and if you do your due diligence and your job well, it is rare that there will be a problem. You'll simply pick up your check after closing and go to the bank.

However, there are normal real estate transaction issues that can create a problem and even kill a deal:

- Bad condition issues not visible in the property but discovered during the inspection by your buyer.
- Undisclosed or undiscovered liens or title issues.
- Seller backs out for whatever reasons.

Don't get too worried, as the condition issues usually are not a problem if you looked the property over carefully. Also, you could have checked courthouse records for liens to avoid that issue.

The learning point here is that the more you do to check out these things before you do an assignment purchase agreement, the less likely you are to run into deal-killing problems.

Why Few Foreclosures or Short Sales?

Banks, lenders and asset managers all want one thing, especially if they're letting a house go at a loss or just a very low price below value. They want a sure thing before they take it off the market.

They are almost never going to accept an assignment contract, as it adds a layer of risk that the property will not close. They have no idea of your experience or if you'll even find a buyer.

Don't worry though, as in the next chapter we'll show you how to fund a deal with transaction funding. It adds complexity, a little risk and extra costs, but it is the only way to work many deals that will not work with an assignment contract.

Chapter 13

Funding When You Need It for a Deal You Can't Pass Up

We've been talking about snap flipping with little or no money of your own or a need for any type of funding. We consider this the absolute best, least risky and highly profitable way to roll deals quickly. However, when lenders or others will not let you use an assignment contract and the deals are too good to pass up, there are options for funding, the money being the missing piece in this snap flip puzzle.

Personal Sources

Before we get into professional lending sources, let's talk about often overlooked resources that you may have available to you personally.

This could be Uncle Fred or any other relative complaining about the return on their investments in stocks, bonds or, worse yet, savings accounts and Certificates of Deposit.

Once you have a track record of successful snap flips, you will undoubtedly be getting some attention from relatives about your great business success. They may approach you, but don't hesitate to approach them for a short-term funding resource for snap flip deals.

Don't consider it going to them hat-in-hand for help. We'll show you in this chapter how to get funding, no matter what your current situation, through transaction lenders. However, why wouldn't you help a relative to triple or more their return on investment and be out of the deal in weeks? They are getting a great deal using you as an investment and you're paying less than the fees of a transaction lender.

This is a business, so approach the loan as a business transaction. Put something in writing, and make sure to cover any tax reporting requirements. You don't want to be paying their taxes later if they do not.

You just may find that, as your success grows, even friends will be eager to invest with you. After all, if they have significant money in a savings account or CD that earns a tiny 3% or so in annual interest, you're able to offer them an amazing improvement.

In fact, it is likely that you can get a relatively inexpensive short term loan and still provide them with a yield of 3% or so for one month! That's 36% on an annual basis, and they're in and out in a hurry.

If you aren't comfortable with this or follow the old adage of do not borrow or lend with relatives, there are other sources we'll talk about here.

Your own savings or equity.

Retirement or Savings Accounts

If you have a 401k, IRA or other retirement account, it is often possible to legally borrow from it for short periods without a tax penalty. Check with your accountant and your retirement plan trustee to see if it will work for you and how to make it happen.

Home Equity

Many investors who have significant equity in their homes are using the HELOC, Home Equity Line of Credit, for a funding resource. It is totally in their control and costs nothing unless you actually use funds.

Shop lenders who advertise HELOC loans for rates and terms. Basically, you get approved for a specified maximum loan amount guaranteed by the equity in your home. This amount is available, but there are no interest or loan costs until you actually access it. You can do this with a check.

When you encounter a great deal and you have a high enough credit line, just write a check to cover the deal and pay it back when your buyer closes on the other end. You'll a pay low interest rate only for the period you have the funds. It's a great solution if your equity is significant.

Cultivated Investors

This is a funding solution that is used less often, but we know of investors who have made it a regular source of funding for their deals. You seek out people who invest in stocks, bonds and other traditional investments. These are people who are not interested in fix & flip or rental property investment.

However, if they are presented with a short term low risk investment that will return double digits, they are going to listen. You can consult an attorney for proper documentation of the relationship so that they hold a stake in the properties until the deal closes on the buyer side. This gives them some protection for their investment.

You would approach these people when you can document multiple snap flip deals that have been profitable for you and that they can verify a very short term situation with a great ROI, Return On Investment. So, what is that return? We would suggest going on to the next section about transaction lending to get some perspective.

Using transaction lenders is expensive, though often the best deals yield enough to use them when it's a choice of transaction lending costs or no deal at all. Once you work up their charges, you can cut them significantly and offer that to these cultivated investors.

You get a better deal and you still offer a great investment to these investors.

Transaction Lenders

Before we get into details, let's review what their role will be, for how much and for how long. You will be in a situation where an assignment contract will not work and it's a great deal. You must in effect buy the house and then resell it to your buyer.

Pros & Cons

Con: Your costs for this type of loan will not be low, but when you can work them in and still get the profit you want, it can be better than walking away from the deal.

Pro: The advantage is that you can build a relationship where you can pretty much count on the money if you meet their requirements for security in the property. They will want their money protected by the value of the property.

Bigger Pro: When you do an assignment contract, this is what the buyer sees and gets. They know what you've negotiated with the seller and they may want to cut into your profits a bit if they think they're excessive. With this type of deal, there are two different purchase contracts, so the buyer doesn't need to know what you paid.

What They're Lending

Within their requirements, they will provide the funds to outright purchase the home. This is necessary due to the mortgage and real estate crash. Before that you could do the "double close" without payment at the first closing.

In other words, you could set up to close on your purchase and fund the buy with the funds from a simultaneous closing by your buyer. It's impossible to do this these days, so here's the way it works:

- You negotiate a purchase price with the seller.
- The transaction lender provides a "proof of funds" for you to present with your offer. This makes banks and lenders happy in the foreclosure market.
- You set up two closings, one for your purchase and the second for your buyer. They are often one right after the other or at least with only a day or two between.

- Your transaction lender funds your purchase.
- When your buyer closes, the transaction loan is paid off and the transaction lender gets their fees. You get what's left.

This is a win-win-win for everybody involved. So, just how much are you going to pay for this type of loan? You'll pay some variation or combination of:

- Loan origination fee
- Interest for time money is in use
- Other fees as itemized

This normally runs into a few thousand dollars on six figure purchases. Costs vary based on experience with your success and the company's own income requirements.

Do you want to make big profits in real estate
without using your own cash?

Use our flash funds as your 'dough for a day,'
and fund all your short sale, REO, and HUD wholesale flips!

These companies are aggressively seeking business, as this screen shot from one of their home pages shows.

The process is an A → B closing and a B → C closing. You are B, A is seller and C is your buyer. The transaction lender funds the A → B closing and get paid back in the B → C closing.

As for what it costs, you won't find hard quotes on many sites. However, one investor who has worked with a lender shared this information in a forum:

Transactional lending is used for a double close. The double close is required when dealing with bank either in a short sale or REO. You would lend the money on the A-B transaction between the bank and the investor.

Typical lender lends at 2% of the purchase plus $250 for "paperwork". Most lenders require a minimum $2500 to do business. You would lend your money for 24-72 hours, then be repaid once the B-C side of the transaction is completed. They lend 100% of the A-B side.

My lender requires:

- A-B Contract
- B-C Contract
- Approval letter from the bank
- Insurance on the property,

Once I send him that, he okays the funds to the title company. He lends with a 72 hour notice.

The promissory note is written such that I do not incur any penalites if the funds are wired back within 72 hours. After 72 hours it is 18% interest rate.

We have resources to help you with creating a relationship with a transactional lender. However, you should do some research on the Internet as well. Then ask us and we can recommend.

The money is out there, so ask for it!

Again, we like the assignment contact quick snap flip best, but some of the best deals would be impossible if you don't have access to funding.

Chapter 14

Pulling it all Together & Your Fee

What you've been learning in this book about our snap flipping strategy is all structured to provide you with a profitable business that requires almost no cash or overhead expense.

We've done a lot of number crunching to determine what our buyer customer can and will pay for the house we deliver. If it's a rental investor, we know we can work with that number, some discount off the current market value for a ready-to-rent home.

However, if it is a fix & flip investor, we must add a layer to our calculations. We still need to know the current market value, or ARV, After Repair Value of the house. The fix & flip investor is usually selling to a rental investor, so we know approximately what their buyer customer will pay.

We then back up from that number to account for the costs of rehab and a profit for the fix & flip investor. It is subjective, as we don't know precisely either number, the rehab cost or the desired profit. We do know that the fix & flip segment of the deal involves some profit in the rehab itself. That investor is marking up the rehab work.

So, what is your value in the deal?

Your investor buyer is willing to pay to compensate you for delivering an investment that will allow them to profit and achieve their desired return on investment. How much they will pay is related to the quality of the investment you deliver. However, there can be limits to how much they think you're worth in relation to what they're getting out of the deal.

We just covered the two ways to handle the double transactions, your buy and your sell side. Either you use an assignment contract or you fund your purchase transaction with borrowed money and pay that back out of your sale closing with the buyer.

The decision as to which approach to take is usually out of your hands. If the seller will not accept an assignment contract, then you must evaluate the deal to see if the reward is worth the costs of transaction funding.

Making up some of the funding cost.

You may be able to make up some or all of the transaction funding costs simply because your buyer is not aware of what you paid for the house. Remember that an assignment contract is passed to your buyer, so they know what you negotiated and may want to bargain with you a bit if you're making a fat profit.

In the case of transaction funding, an entirely new purchase agreement is executed for the sale to your buyer, so they only have that price as a reference. They are only evaluating the deal based on that price and their investment goals. You may be able to offset some or all of the transaction funding costs with a higher sale price.

Value is in the eye of the beholder.

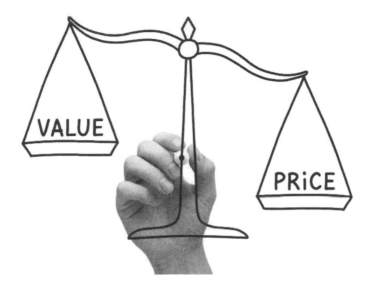

To illustrate a point about value versus price when working with your buyers, let's back up to the time and effort that we've invested in building our buyer list. Not only that, but what is an active investor repeat buyer worth to you?

You've networked and advertised, and will continually do so, to add buyers to your database. They are valuable to your business. The better the deals you deliver, the more valuable you become to their businesses.

With all of this in mind, weigh the value to you of a big strike on one deal versus eager buyers calling to ask when you're going to have another deal for them. If you are getting eager repeat business, you gain some valuable benefits:

- You enter negotiations with your sellers knowing you have a strong buyer demand backing you up.
- Being a little more conservative in your profit requirements can mean multiple buyers for single properties, which runs the price up anyway.

What you're trying to do is to maximize your profit from each deal, but balance that with the value of eager buyers who welcome your next deal and even compete for it.

There are snap flippers out there who settle into great relationships with just a few happy buyers and even agree up front to certain profit margins for the right deals that meet buyer requirements.

If you want to get excited, have a buyer tell you they'll take every deal you bring them that meets their requirements. You know the neighborhoods they buy in, the discount they want off market value, and the rents/cash flows they want from their investments. When you find a deal that works, you can confidently negotiate to fill the standing order.

Snap Flipping Reviewed

To wind this up, let's do a review of the snap flipping strategy. We'll run through the high points in the book to pull together a process flow that you can use as a quick outline and flow from a desire to make money through snap flipping to a profitable business.

Before that, let's make one point. This book is a thorough treatment of the concept and process of snap flipping. Think of it as a college class on snap flipping. However, if you were in a real estate college and could major in snap flipping, there would be lots more to learn to get your degree and become an expert.

You can just jump right in and get started, and we even encourage you to do so. Start locating buyers for your database. You should devote as much time and effort as necessary to locate and start relationships with as many active real estate investors as possible.

While you're doing that, look at our course offerings, seminars and recommended resources. Getting more specific knowledge under your belt is never wasted effort. When you get your buyer list to the point of finding deals, you want to come out of the starting gate with a winning attitude and the knowledge to back it up.

The Buyer List

We like to call it a database, just to reinforce the requirement that you must record information about your buyers.

- Neighborhoods in which they are interested.
- Price ranges of homes of interest.
- If rental investors, their cash flow requirements.
- Learn enough investment math to think like a rental property investor.
- If fix & flip investors, their desired profit margins & how they figure rehab costs.
- How fast the can or want to move to close a deal.

Those are the major items you want to know about your buyers. If you don't know enough about what they want, you will be approaching them with properties in which they have no interest.

Doing the Fix & Flip Calculations

To approach your fix & flip buyers with deals they will want, you need to learn what you can about the rehab estimation process. You can rely on others, but since you're not hiring anyone, don't count on getting free bids for very long.

- Locate and learn to use an online or other solution to quickly arrive at reasonable estimates for renovation and repair work.
- Assume the fix & flip investor's profit is partly marking up the rehab costs and then adding to them as much as they can get and still have a willing buyer.

As you do deals, you'll become good at this, but it will never be anything but estimates. Spending your time and effort in becoming a better negotiator and locating deals where you can buy with really deep discounts is how you'll overcome most miscalculation in these rehab estimates.

Build a system to locate deals & motivated sellers

Here is where you can use online and software resources to deliver information to you in an efficient way. The more you take advantage of technology to bring properties to your attention the better.

Work on systems that help you to cull through the many properties that will come into your funnel to only spend your valuable evaluation time on the ones most likely to be real deals. Use tools to file information and quickly retrieve it when you need it.

Prepare and negotiate as a business person.

Once you locate a property that could work into a deal, you want to go into your negotiation with the seller with the proper preparation.

Your preparations and strategy for a foreclosure are very different than those in negotiating with an owner. We outlined an approach for foreclosures, and understand that any tactic is a good one. Your goal is to drive that lender or asset manager to the absolute lowest dollar, and hurting their feelings isn't going to happen.

In negotiating with an owner, you are working with some level of distress and possibly time pressures. Explain to them how you do business and that you deliver deals to buyers so must meet their requirements. Your value to them is in getting them out from under their house and letting them move on.

Choose the transaction process/funding

You may make an early decision in your business plan to only do assignment contract deals, and that would be fine. It will limit the deal types and the number of deals you may be able to put together. However, if you laser focus on assignment deals, it can be highly profitable.

However, if you are locating deals with lenders or other sellers who will not accept an assignment contract, build your funding resources so you're ready to take advantage of them.

Get Started on Assembly Line Profits

You're ready to get started. Sure, some more education and research is in order. However, getting started on meeting buyers is a non-threatening first step. Don't hesitate… you're ready.

NOTES

NOTES

NOTES

NOTES

NOTES